j602
H73s

W9-BXF-683

AGD6384-8

CL
6/99

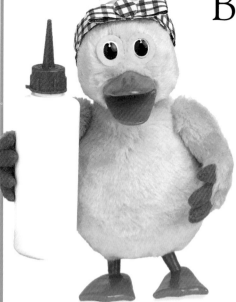

Before you start ...

1 Gather together everything you need for the activity using the equipment list at the top of each page. You can use white glue for all the activities in this book.

2 Cover your worktable with newspaper and wear an apron to protect your clothes.

3 Read all the instructions carefully. Always wait for glue to dry.

4 Be very careful with scissors. Only use them if an adult is there to help you.

5 When you have finished an activity, wash your hands and put everything away.

A DK PUBLISHING BOOK

Written and edited by Lara Tankel and Dawn Sirett
Art Editors Mandy Earey and Mary Sandberg
Additional design Veneta Altham
Deputy Managing Art Editor C. David Gillingwater
US Editor Camela Decaire
Production Fiona Baxter
Dib, Dab, and Dob made by Wilfrid Wood
Photography by Alex Wilson and Norman Hollands
Illustrations by Peter Kavanagh
Frieze, masks, dragon, and collage made by Jane Bull

First American Edition, 1997
2 4 6 8 10 9 7 5 3 1

Published in the United States by DK Publishing, Inc.
95 Madison Avenue, New York, New York 10016

Copyright © 1997 Dorling Kindersley Limited, London
Visit us on the World Wide Web at http://www.dk.com

All rights reserved. No part of this publication may be reproduced, stored in a retrieval system, or transmitted in any form or by any means, electronic, mechanical, photocopying, recording, or otherwise, without the prior written permission of the copyright owner.

Published in Great Britain by Dorling Kindersley Ltd.

A CIP catalog record for this book is available from the Library of Congress.

ISBN 0-7894-1520-8

Color reproduction by Colourscan, Singapore
Printed and bound in Hong Kong by Imago

PLAY AND LEARN

Sticking Things

With Dib, Dab, and Dob

black
construction paper scissors cellophane
candy wrappers white
glue

Make stained-glass pictures

Ask an adult to fold
a square of paper in
quarters and to
cut out shapes
along the
folded edges.

Fold the paper
again and cut
out more shapes.

Then open up
the paper and
glue candy
wrappers
over all
the holes.

long strip of cardboard   pencil   white glue   glitter

Sprinkle glitter fish on a frieze

Draw fish, waves, and seaweed on a strip of cardboard.

Carefully spread glue along the lines you have drawn.

Then sprinkle glitter over the glue.

flowers
and leaves
 notebook
 white
glue
paintbrush

Cover a notebook with flowers

Glue flowers and
leaves onto the front
of a notebook with
white glue.

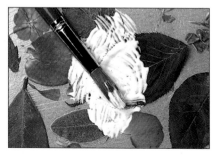

Brush the glue
all over the notebook
and over the flowers
and leaves, too.

Design happy animal masks

Draw an oval mask with eyeholes on cardboard. Glue felt to the cardboard and then cut out the mask.

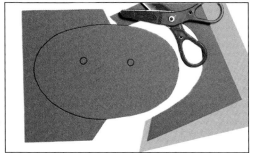

Cut out the eyeholes. Check that you can see through them.

tape   elastic thread

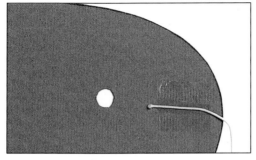

Tape the ends of a length of elastic thread to the back of the mask on each side.

I've made frog eyes by sticking felt pieces onto cardboard.

Then glue on felt pieces to make an animal face.

Funny felt faces

Try making lots of masks for all
your friends to wear at a party.

Glue scales on a fiery dragon

Draw a dragon on some paper.

Choose pages from a magazine. Tear them into small squares and glue them onto the dragon.

Glue on strips of tissue paper for the dragon's fiery breath.

The paper squares look like the dragon's scaly skin.

Make a farm collage

Find things that you can use to make a farm picture. Cut them into the shapes you want.

Arrange them on a sheet of cardboard.

cardboard

white glue

Then glue the things onto the cardboard.

Feely farm picture

Glue strips of cardboard
around the edge of the
picture to make a frame.

The cotton
sheep feel soft
and fluffy. The
bark feels bumpy
and rough.